D1330548

OUT OF PRINT
HELD AT
LAST COPY STORE

County
Store

591.18

www.hants.gov.uk/library

 Hampshire
County Council

 Love
YOUR LIBRARY

Tel: 0300 555 1387

HAMPSHIRE COUNTY LIBRARY
WITHDRAWN.

C014330746

DELIRIOUS DENIM
© 2007 by Liaoning Science and Technology Press

**First published in the UK by Southbank Publishing 2007
21 Great Ormond Street, London WC1N 3JB**

www.southbankpublishing.com

Authors	: Luo Lv
	Zhang Huiguang
Editor	: Xu Guiying
Editor (English edition)	: Melody Tan
Project manager	: Dawn Teo
Cover design	: Beverly Chong
Designers	: Zhang Huiguang
	Xie Jing

All rights reserved. No part of this book may be reproduced, stored in or introduced into a retrieval system, or transmitted, in any form or by any means (electronic, mechanical, photocopying, recording or otherwise) without the written permission of the publishers.

Any person who does any unauthorised act in relation to this publication may be liable to criminal prosecution and civil claims for damages.

A CIP catalogue record for this book is available from the British Library.

**ISBN 10: 1-904915-25-6
ISBN 13: 978-1-904915-25-6**

2 4 6 8 10 9 7 5 3 1

Printed by SNP Leefung Printers (Shenzen) Co Ltd, China

DELIRIOUS DENIM

southbank
publishing

CONTENTS

005

HAMPSHIRE COUNTY LIBRARY	
C014330746	
HJ	11/12/2007
R391.009	£19.99
9781904915256	

FOREWORD

Despite being invented in the late 1800s, denim jeans have withstood the test of time and the fickleness of trends to remain an important part of people's lives today. From their beginnings more than a century ago, jeans have come a long way from the mines to the catwalk, crossing boundaries of class, age and nationality, and are embraced for their unmatched comfort and appeal. They have become an enduring style icon that is still very much relevant today.

What is the story behind the blue denim that has captured the hearts (and legs) of people all over the world?

ill Powers.   Bob Dalton.   Gr

006

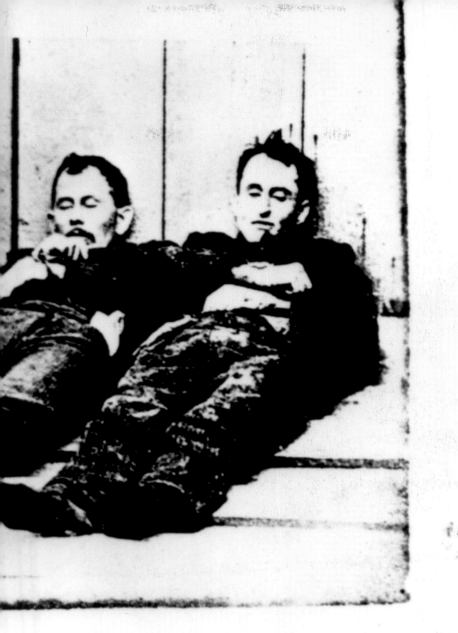

t Dalton.   Dick Brodwel

Texas Jack

Chapter I The Legend of Denim

The first pair of jeans

Although there have been different stories about how jeans came about more than a century ago, both Strauss and Nevada tailor Jacob Davis are always mentioned in stories and records.

When it comes to the birth of the first pair of jeans, the name, Levi Strauss, will inevitably be mentioned. Strauss is universally recognised as the inventor of jeans – people even called him Mr Jeans.

Mining was hard work and often resulted in torn britches

Jeans first became popular with miners because of their durability and hardiness

It is said that when German immigrant Levi Strauss opened his dry goods wholesale company in San Francisco in 1853, at the height of the Gold Rush, he found miners complaining about their easily torn cotton britches and pockets that "split right out", spilling the ore that miners stored inside. So Strauss came up with the idea of making rugged overalls from the canvas he originally brought over to sell as tent cloth. The miners were very excited and satisfied with the new trousers, which held up very well. Some say that this innovation only came about because Strauss was desperate to dispose of his canvas, which was not selling well. Nevertheless, these trousers were a great success.

Although Strauss played a big part, the birth of the jeans we know today could also not have happened without Jacob Davis, who was a tailor in a small shop in Nevada.

Back in 1860, as one story goes, Alkali Ike, a miner in the Comstock mining camp in Nevada, often complained to Davis, his tailor, that his trousers were always torn apart while mining ore. Others believe that in 1870, Davis's neighbour wanted him to make a pair of durable trousers for her husband, who worked as a lumberman. In both stories, Davis came upon the idea of adding copper rivets, which were usually used to make saddles, to the corners of the pockets, so that they would be stronger.

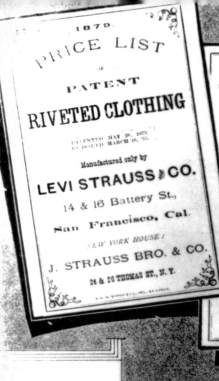

1879.

PRICE LIST

of

PATENT

RIVETED CLOTHING

PATENTED MAY 20, 1873
RE-ISSUED MARCH 16, '75.

Manufactured only by

LEVI STRAUSS & CO.

14 & 16 Battery St.,

San Francisco, Cal.

NEW YORK HOUSE:

J. STRAUSS BRO. & CO.

24 & 26 THOMAS ST., N.Y.

PANTS AND VESTS.

		PER DOZ.
RIVETED	Brown, Mode and Dead Grass, best 10 oz. Duck Pants	$16 50
"	Brown, Mode and Dead Grass, best 10 oz. Duck Pants EXTRA SIZES...........	20 00
"	Amoskeag Blue Denim Pants..	15 50
"	XX Extra Heavy Blue Denim Pants	17 50
"	XX Extra Heavy Blue Denim Pants, EXTRA SIZES.....	21 00
"	Brown, Mode and Dead Grass, best 10 oz. Duck Pants, (YOUTHS')	15 00
"	XX Extra Heavy Blue Denim Pants (YOUTHS')	15 50
"	Blanket Lined Brown, Mode and Dead Grass, best 10 oz. Duck Pants	35 00
"	Canton Flannel Lined, Brown, Mode and Dead Grass, best 10 oz. Duck Pants.	22

	Brown, Mode and Dead Grass, best 10 oz. Duck Hunting Vest...............	19
"	Blanket Lined, Brown, Mode and Dead Grass, best 10 oz. Duck Vests...............	22 50

A Discount to the Trade.

PATENTED MAY 28
RE-ISSUED MARCH 1

PANTS.

BLANKET LINED AND

Back

VESTS.

BLANKET LINED AND UNL

Back   Front

HUNTING COATS.

Front

Back

Front

BLOUSES.

BLANKET LINED AND UNLINED.

Front

Back

Levi Strauss, the founder of Levi Strauss & Co.

He wrote to Strauss, his fabric supplier, on 5 July 1872, claiming to be the inventor of riveted trousers and suggesting that the company should share the patent with him. He also sent two samples of the trousers, one of white cotton canvas and the other of blue denim, along with the letter.

In 1873, rivets were added to the back pockets of Levi's jeans to make them stronger

It is difficult to get a definite account on the birth of jeans. The only proof is of the letter from Davis to Strauss, and their registration for the patent for riveted trousers, which was granted to them in 1873. The production of riveted trousers began in 1876, and the history of jeans was made.

Where do jeans come from?

It is widely believed that the name "jeans" comes from a kind of endurable trousers called *genoese* or *genes*, which were the uniform for sailors in the Italian port city, Genova. From the etymological point of view, "jean" is from the Italian word "da Genova". Other experts, who carried out further study of the word, declared that it is the American spelling for *genois*, which refers to a kind of canvas. The canvas was used for work-wear from the late 19th century, but the name "jeans" had not been widely used until 1920. They were usually called riveted trousers or waist overalls.

Blue jeans are still a classic favourite

Jeans thrived in the American West

Indigo denim

At first, the canvas used for the riveted trousers was thick and hard, and by no means comfortable. This was a disturbing problem for Strauss. He later found a kind of blue and white fabric sold on the European market, which was both strong and soft. He immediately imported some. This fabric, called *serge*, was made in a small French town, and was referred to as *serge de Nîmes* (serge cloth from Nîmes). But when the cloth arrived in Britain, the British businessmen found it difficult to pronounce its name, hence they called it "denim" for short.

Denim is a cotton twill fabric that is dyed with indigo, a natural dye from plants. The woven fabric is comprised of dyed warp threads, the lengthwise threads, and plain weft thread, the crosswise threads. As the indigo could only dye the surface of the thread, the colour would fade with time and use. Hence irregular fading and abrasion would appear, giving the fabric a unique style.

With the production of synthetic indigo in the early 1900s, cheap blue jeans became more and more popular. This wide acceptance is closely connected with the relationship between the colour blue and work-wear. As early as the 17th century, indigo was widely used as a dye for work-wear in Europe. So for the Europeans who emigrated to America at that time, the familiar blue indigo colour was easily accepted. Blue denim work trousers became quite common for workers and indigo blue became the standard colour for Levi's jeans.

The "jeans" look

It is said that the original design of jeans was inspired by the leotards of Texas cowboys, which featured narrow hips, low waists and straight legs. In Levi's jeans, then, an orange-brown cotton thread was used, which left a conspicuous outer seam line. There were also five pockets, with each corner strengthened by rivets, and a zip that fastened the front. Later on, to build up the company image, several symbolic images were used on its jeans, namely the Arcuate stitch, leather patch and red tab. Today, the familiar standard for jeans remains as indigo denim, external stitching, red tabs and leather patches.

Jeans captured the American rodeo cowboy spirit

CHECK BLOTTER, 1940s

In 1939, Lee teamed up with *Ripley's Believe It Or Not!* to create a series of advertisements showing the strength and success of Lee jeans and their wearers

Through the ages

The 20th century was an eventful period, most notably for the two World Wars and the Great Depression. In one way or another, jeans made their presence felt during these times.

The period of war ironically enhanced the popularity of jeans. In World War I, jeans were designated by the American federal government as the uniform for their troops. Lee's Union All was the chosen working uniform for soldiers, and even women who were in the military were asked to wear the same uniform. As a result of these developments, jeans became more common after the war, especially for women.

Norman Rockwell's painting, *Rosie the Riveter*, was used as a symbol of patriotism in the Saturday Evening Post in 1943

In 1926, the zip, invented by Whitcomb Judson in 1893, was used by Lee to create the first zipped jeans. While the men's jeans were zipped in front, women's jeans were zipped at the side as it was considered unacceptable otherwise. But 50 years later, Lee Cooper revolutionised women's jeans by zipping them in the front. His practice has continued to today.

041

In the 1930s, America faced the Great Depression. Richer Americans from the East could no longer afford the luxurious European holidays that they had enjoyed before. So they holidayed in the American West instead. Gradually, the beautiful Western plains as well as the handsome cowboys in jeans that they saw in movies became more and more appealing. Tourists also brought jeans home as a souvenir of their time in the American West. At the same time, horsemanship competitions that were popular then also helped to make jeans more acceptable. Consumers across America started to use jeans as casual wear.

In May 1935, Levi's advertised its ladies jeans for the first time in American magazine *Vogue*. Two Western girls wore jeans and posed attractively. Levi's wanted to emphasise the aesthetic aspects of jeans rather than their work-wear practicality. Jeans were no longer just tough, they could be modern and charming as well. Since then, jeans have become a fashion item and have entered the daily life of Americans.

The

PATRONIZE YOUR HOM

est grew up in Levi's

MERCHANT — HE'S YOUR NEIGHBOR

LEVI'S
AMERICA'S FINEST
OVERALL
SINCE 1850

{ 1926 cowboy overalls }

{ 1950s / 1960s Levi's
blue jeans }

{ waist overalls from
the Calico Mine }

{ 1939 waist overalls }

Riding boots were the perfect shoes to go with jeans in the past

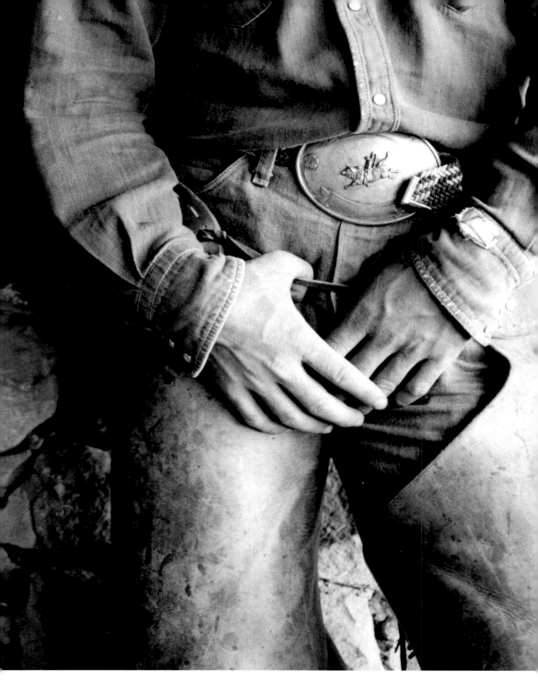

The cowboy look

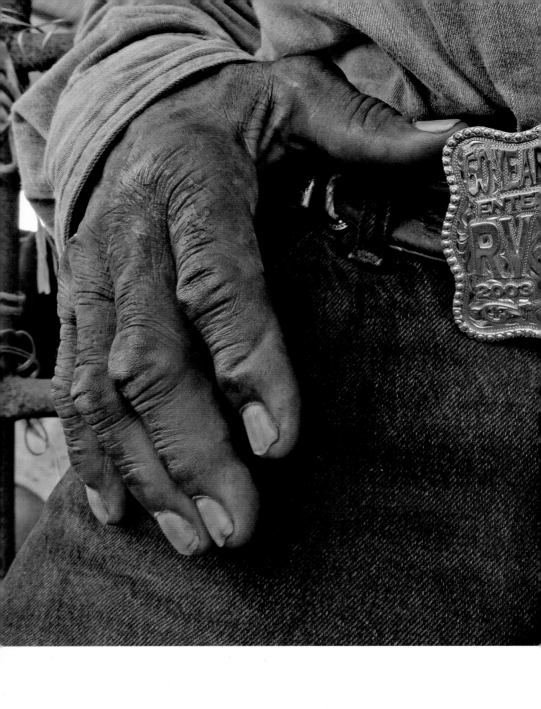

For almost a decade, discrimination and lack of funding kept Black Rodeo Cowboys out of the rodeo limelight. Now on any given Sunday afternoon from February to November, within a 60-mile radius of Houston, Texas, black cowboys can be found competing in all-black rodeos

Cowboy boots with spurs

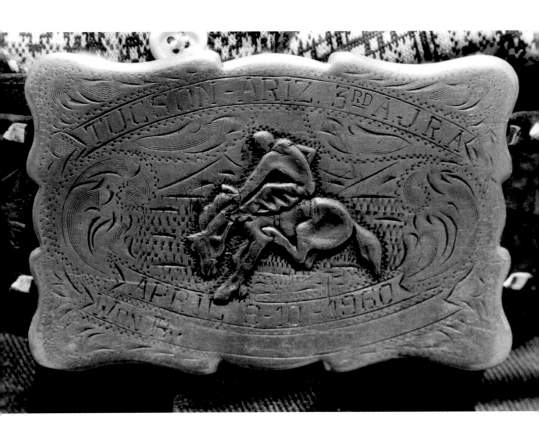

The cowboy life has a particular appeal. Whether it be herding cattle, managing a ranch or taming wild horses, they all share a common thirst for adventure and solitude

An American family in jeans in a 1943 advertisement for war bonds

As America prepared for battle during World War II, colourful propaganda posters were circulated, in which jeans appeared as the symbol of unity and Americanness. In an advertisement in 1943, a family stood in front of the stars and stripes, calling out to fellow Americans to buy war bonds and support the government. Every single one of them wore blue jeans.

Levi's 501 jeans were also given to soldiers as necessities during the war. When the war ended, the soldiers went back home, disposing of large quantities of their Levi's jeans in Europe, where they had landed to help the Allied forces. The jeans were sold to the locals and this was the start of the jeans fever in Europe. On top of that, European uniform makers began to imitate the American worker uniform: jeans. As a result, almost every European had a pair of jeans after the war.

Due to the overwhelming demand around the world, jeans used to be a major product in the black market between America, the former USSR and the Third World.

LEVI'S

AUTHENTIC
WESTERN SHIRTS

UNTER CARD, 1940s

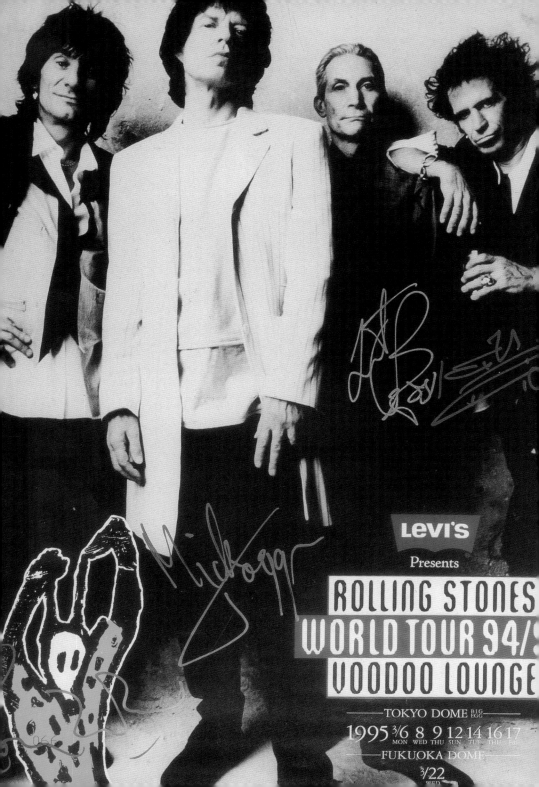

Hollywood and popular culture

Following the economic recovery after the war, American popular culture blossomed. In the 1950s, the most popular films in theatres were *A Streetcar Named Desire* (1951), *The Wild One* (1953), *River of No Return* (1954) and *Rebel Without a Cause* (1955). These films shot stars like James Dean, Marlon Brando and Marilyn Monroe to fame. Images of celebrities in jeans were everywhere in magazines and weeklies. For some time, the hottest look was straight jeans worn with a T-shirt and jacket. As more and more American movies were exported to Europe, the jeans culture also influenced European youths.

James Dean in jeans

The Hillbilly Cat : Elvis Presley

While jeans were part of the American popular culture, they were also equated with rebellion and anti-tradition in the 1960s. Young people used jeans as a tool to express their discontentment with society. When America started the Vietnam War, many youths participated in the anti-war movement. In an anti-war congregation at the University of California, Berkeley, jeans were the uniform. In the anti-war concert in Woodstock, almost all the 400,000 young men and women were in jeans.

Hippies first emerged in San Francisco in the late 1960s, and soon the rebellious wave swept through Europe. Similar groups appeared in Britain, France, Italy, East Europe, and even Japan. Jeans played an important role and sent an important message to the world for these youths — they were anti-establishment, independent and would do whatever they wanted.

American street style is about wearing jeans with personality

By then, the style of jeans had also varied greatly. Flared jeans became popular and their flares were unprecedentedly wide. Members of the famous pop band The Beatles favoured this style, helping to spread it all over Europe as well. Jeans also came in wide varieties of decorations, fabrics and colours. Stonewash began around this time and was used by Nudie Cohen, the famous Hollywood "rodeo tailor". This effect was achieved by washing a light floatstone together with the jeans, giving the jeans a worn-in look through the resulting friction. The invention of floatstone-ground jeans cannot be separated from the French jeans brand Marithé and François Girbaud, which was founded by Marithé Bachellerie and François Girbaud in 1964. The couple wanted to reflect their humanitarian ideas through the fabric and transfer their thoughts through the cut of the garment. They constantly found ways to sew more innovatively and to change the fixed look of jeans. In 1965, they decided to change the style of jeans by stonewashing them. They added detritus when washing the pre-treated jeans, giving the jeans a special effect in colour and texture. This was warmly welcomed by jeans fans. However, stonewashing only gained widespread popularity when Lee began to use it in 1982.

Stonewashed jeans are popular among youths and jam bands because of their added character

Going mainstream

Thanks to Hollywood stars and popular culture like rock music, punk and pop art, jeans had become part of mainstream fashion, and not just for the middle and working classes. Even fashion designers had begun to take notice of it – jeans appeared in Yves Saint Laurent's fashion show and Pierre Cardin's costume press conference. Jeans were also found in the wardrobes of royalty and politicians. Princess Anne of Britain, Georges Pompidou, ex-president of France, and America's former presidents Jimmy Carter and Ronald Reagan were all seen in jeans. Jimmy Carter used to campaign during the presidential elections in jeans, and Ronald Reagan's love for jeans was very much in line with what he called himself, a "citizen politician".

At the end of the 1970s, jeans came into the lives of the Chinese as the China market gradually opened up. However, it still required a lot of courage for a young Chinese person to swagger through the streets in jeans at that time.

Jeans are now a fashion norm in popular culture

The socio-cultural phenomenon of jeans was also given much attention at that time. In newspapers, magazines and television shows, it was constantly being analysed, reviewed and discussed. Shows and exhibitions were held from New York to Paris. In 1973, the show named "Rebirth of the Blues. A Denim Art Show" was held in New York. Exhibitions about denim jeans were also held in many European cities, like "Indigo, Leven in een Kleur" at the Tropical Museum in Amsterdam in 1985; "Blu Blue-Jeans: Il Blu Popolare" in Saint George Genoa in 1989; and "Arts and Jeans: Reliefs Minimaux, Passage de Retz" in Paris in 1994. Jeans were no longer just about fashion, but were also valuable items that were culturally important enough to be viewed and appreciated in museums. In fact, several original Levi's 501 jeans were already part of the permanent collection in the Smithsonian Museum in Washington DC back in 1976, as part of that year's commemoration of America's 200th National Day.

Jeans have evolved from being work-wear to being haute couture.
Shown in the picture is Italian brand Energie's new skinny jeans

Ups and downs

Though jeans have never been totally cast aside, they have experienced ups and downs in the fashion world. In spite of the initial furore over jeans, they declined in popularity until the 1980s, when interest in jeans surged again because of the introduction of designer jeans. But the attitude towards jeans had changed in the West – there was more focus on the versatility and workmanship of jeans, and quality was valued over quantity. Famous brands like Levi's had no choice but to cut back on production. In the mid 1980s, Levi's began heavy advertising on the classic look. Traditional five-pocket jeans, red line selvage jeans and jeans with copper rivets instead of zips became the in-thing once again. Other jeans companies eagerly followed suit, extending the trend to the 1990s. By the late 1980s, all kinds of whimsical designs, such as drop-waist styles, cuffed legs and floral embroidery, declared that jeans were all about individualism.

When it came to the 1990s, retro fever was in vogue with flared trousers and blue denim making a comeback. Whether it was in the streets of New York or Tokyo, people dressed themselves in the way that jeans were originally worn when they first appeared in the US – large, loose and hanging at the hips. As the 1990s came to an end, the reconsideration of values and the attention paid to environment protection meant that jeans were worn pure and plain. Red line selvage, no stonewash and second-hand jeans became great hits, and young men and women searched high and low for vintage jeans that were no longer in production.

RESERVED FOR PINK PE

RES

Chapter II The Blooming Age

The story behind the brand

In 1853, Levi Strauss set up Levi Strauss & Co. (LS&CO.) in San Francisco, a city swept by the Gold Rush. Then on 20 May 1873, together with Nevada tailor Jacob Davis, Strauss got the patent for using copper rivets for men's work trousers. This date is considered the official birthday of "blue jeans".

The four hallmarks of Levi's

Copper rivet

The copper rivet has been an indispensable part of Levi's jeans since Jacob started adding rivets to them. The rivets were used to strengthen the trousers. Since then, rivets of different materials have been used. Originally, the rivets were an alloy of copper and steel and would scratch horse saddles and other furniture when they were attached to the hip pockets. So Levi's tried wrapping the rivets in the jeans fabric. But when cowboys sat before the fire, the wrapped rivets still made them uncomfortable because they got hot quickly. In 1937, Levi's began to strengthen the pocket corners, front edges, belt holes and zips by corner seaming instead of rivets. By 1966, the rivets on the pockets had all been removed. Only the rivets on the front pockets have remained to today.

Arcuate stitch

The Arcuate stitch on the hip pockets of Levi's jeans is considered to be the world's earliest trademark for clothing. In the past, the Arcuate stitching design was made with a single needle application, and each design was unique, depending on the skill of the person sewing it. Today, the design is uniform because a double-needle machine is used. This machine is also responsible for the "diamond" shape at the point where the two lines of stitching meet.

In 1943, Levi's registered the Arcuate stitching design as its trademark. The double-bird image was meant to represent the spirit of freedom. It was said to be inspired by a rare bird flying into Strauss's shop and landing on the hip pockets of the jeans way back in 1873.

L E V I ' S. L A D Y   S T Y L E

Leather patch

Legend has it that Levi's agreed to put its jeans to the test – a pair of jeans were pulled by two horses which were running in opposite directions. It turned out that the jeans were so strong that even two horses could not tear them apart.

Over the years, Levi's has tried using different materials like cattle hide and canvas for the leather patch, to make it suitable for washing in washing machines.

Although the story of the Levi's test may very well be a myth, the leather label of a pair of jeans in between two horses is still being sewn now onto every single pair of jeans, signifying the confident guarantee of quality by Levi's.

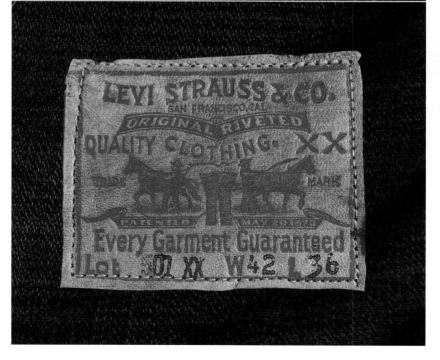

The Levi's red tab has evolved from its first appearance in 1936

Red tab

To stand out in an increasingly competitive market, Levi's started attaching a little red cloth with the Levi's brand name sewn on it on the hip pockets of its jeans. This red tab has been sewn on the upper side of all hip pockets since 1936.

The footprints of Levi's

Due to the rationing of essential items like thread in World War II, Levi's had to paint on the Arcuate stitch design on its back pockets. Customers thought that the jeans were fakes and refused to buy them. The Arcuate stitch reappeared in 1947 after the war ended.

Levi's also had to remove the flaps on the jeans pockets, as flapless jeans shaped and fitted the hips much better and became more favoured among customers. Also, because of the fact that denim shrank in the wash, many young men became attracted by this new sexy work-wear.

The 1960's were a Golden Age for Levi's. Its business in Europe expanded greatly and its profits and fame soared. In 1960, Levi's came out with wheat-coloured jeans, and in 1964, the first Sta-Prest (intended to be pronounced as "stay pressed") series of wrinkle-free trousers was introduced. They were supposed to be wearable right out of the dryer, with no need for ironing. This series catered to both the hippies and the yuppies of that era, improving versatility for the hippies, but at the same time, being decent enough for the yuppies. By the end of the 1960s, the baby-boomer generation was a huge market and Levi's was able to capitalise on that as a symbol of fashion and youth.

In 1971, Levi's went public and bought up companies such as Perry Ellis, Oxford Suits and women's clothing manufacturer, Koret, to diversify its business. This turned out to be a mistake. After considering the Levi's business and tradition, the Haas family, who played an increasingly important role in the company, decided to privatise the company. They sold all the non-jeans sections to shift the company's focus back on jeans.

The Levi's factory in the 1960s

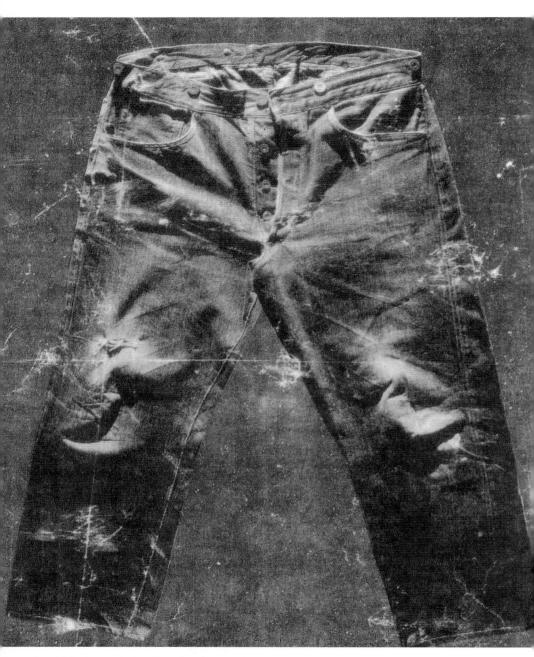

In 1986, Levi's launched the "Dust Storm" series of pre-washed jeans in warm cast denim

Levi's witnessed another turning point in 1986. The century-old brand resolvedly abandoned the amiable image that it had always held, introducing the Dust Storm series of pre-washed jeans in warm cast denim. They were displayed everywhere on shop counters, which caused a sensation among youths. Their parents, the old Levi's fans, were shocked. It was the first time that Levi's had subverted its concept of classic jeans and tried to keep up with the young generation. But at that time there were more than three million youths aged from 12 to 19 years old, who would spend more than a third of their money on clothes. And Levi's needed them.

Despite the surge in popularity in the past decades, jeans became less and less sought after in the 1990s, and domestic sales went downhill. Jeans were no longer considered front runners in fashion. Robert Haas, who had a Harvard MBA and previously served in the Peace Corps as well as McKinsey & Co., took over as CEO. He began to carry out his strategy of winning over the global market with the goal of Levi's being a global clothing manufacturer in mind. In foreign markets, the company daringly propagandised American culture, making it synonymous with fashion amongst European and Asian customers. The brave and creative marketing tactics yielded results. Though domestic sales were shrinking, overseas markets were helping the company grow. By then, Levi Strauss & Co., the company that is a fixture in American history and culture, also became a large global brand.

The 3D Engineered Jeans launched in 2000 were another milestone in the history of Levi's. They were a hit with youths everywhere. The three, rather than two-dimensional tailoring gave the denim a strong cubic effect. Moreover, a starched effect was also added to the cloth. In 2003, the new Type 1 Jeans had much creative work on its details: the copper rivets, red tab, leather patch, copper button and Arcuate stitch were enlarged by several times. To remain relevant in fashion, Levi's had to continually innovate and surprise.

Levi's 501

Lynn Downey, the historian for Levi Strauss & Co., once re-marked that of all the vintage series, only the 501 can be truly valuable. What makes the 501 so charming?

501®
STAY TRUE

119

Normally, a pair of classic 501 jeans needs a piece of denim cloth about 1.6 metres long, a 191-metre-long sewing thread, five buttons, six copper rivets and 37 independent tailoring procedures. From 1873 to 2003, Levi's developed 13 different styles of 501 jeans. But the original features of jeans as work-wear – the anti-fit straight cut, square, loose and comfortable design, and fitting mid-waist cubic cut – were retained. These perfectly display the unique charm of classic straight jeans. Since jeans would shrink in the wash, the shrink-to-fit method was used so that the high quality clingy fabric would become softer, more comfortable and more fitting with each wash. The colour of the jeans would also fade a little each time. Another indispensable characteristic of 501 jeans is their button fly, which replaced zips.

The 501 series is the most representative of all Levi's jeans. In the 1970s, almost every young man had at least one pair of 501 jeans. Levi's even held a jeans-painting competition, inviting people to send in their works of grease-painted 501 jeans. The competition committee received 10,000 pieces altogether. The winners' works are still on exhibition in museums all around America.

5
0 1.®

501®
STAY TRUE

Levi's

On the wall of the Levi's headquarters are the following words: empathy, originality, integrity and courage. They are both the guidelines for the company's staff and the reasons underlying a century of quality. Consistent with the values of the company, the Levi Strauss Foundation was established in 1952. This independent foundation provides grants to many organisations which need help. It offers an annual global grant budget of about US$15 million to help alleviate poverty and discrimination for women and youths. Levi's has since become an American tradition, symbolic of Western strength and spirit.

Brands galore

Over the last century, jeans brands have mushroomed one after another. Facing fierce competition, each brand has had to assert themselves with their own distinct characteristics.

The first gallus overalls by Lee in 1911

Lee 1889

In the long history of the jeans evolution from work-wear to fashion wear, Lee, the second biggest American brand, has played a very important role. Henry David Lee set up his H. D. Lee Mercantile Company in Kansas in 1889. Originally, the company mainly dealt with selling work trousers, and in 1911, it made its first work-wear jeans. Some of Lee's classical styles, like Big Overall and Union All, are still popular these days. Big Overalls were the first suspender trousers and Union All was the uniform for the American soldiers during World War I. These styles are commonly seen in old movies.

Lee decided to bid farewell to work-wear in 1924, and focused its attention on making "American jeans". It began to produce jeans in denim that was 13 times heavier than common denim, and added copper rivets to the jeans. Its new product was called Lee Riders. In 1926, Lee initiated the world's first zipped jeans and managed to design a very comfortable U-saddle style. It also popularised the concept of "made to measure" jeans, which made it possible for the brand to be both practical and fashionable. After World War II, Lee moved in on the Eastern American cities as its jeans became more and more popular. At the same time, Lee's leather series was introduced, which together with the success of Lee Rider, established its role as a classic brand. Lee made another breakthrough in the jeans world, launching women's jeans, which put an end to jeans made solely for men. With Lee's "fit for girls" series, a new page was turned in the history of women's jeans.

Since 1986, Lee has been catering to customers of different ages with its different series of jeans. Lee Basic was a series of classic five-pocket styles matched with different cuts from different trends; Chinos-Lee was a casual wear series; and Rough Rider was a high quality traditional series which had a fashionable cut and a packing method that made it the symbol of Lee's product guarantee and market image. In the 1980s, Lee made the world's biggest jeans, the 23-metre-high Lee 101Z, which were listed in the *Guinness Book of Records*. And in 1995, Lee became the first American jeans brand to enter the Chinese market.

Sally O'Sullivan
ROBBIE WILLIAMS'
FAN MAIL COORDINATOR

Lee BEHIND THE SCENES
SINCE 1889

chad taylor
KYLIE MINOGUE'S
PET CARE DIRECTOR

Lee BEHIND THE SCENES
SINCE 1889

Though it was 40 years younger than jeans pioneer Levi's, Lee turned out to be a challenging rival, booming in a market of fierce competition and being well-loved by female customers. Lee's success is exemplified in its classic ad slogan, "The brand that fits". Lee wisely opened up the female market in a male-dominated jeans world, making women its target. It abandoned the straight cut of jeans and tried to complement the curviness of a woman's figure, setting it apart from other jeans and earning its place in the wardrobes of many women. Up until today, Lee's long history has made it one of the main brands in American jeans. Lee has a firm hold in both the old fashion world and in the avant-garde frontier. Both traditional and fashionable, Lee has become an icon for jeans.

Wrangler 1904

Black jeans are the most remarkable contribution that Wrangler made to the history of jeans. When introduced to customers in 1904 by Blue Bell Company, black jeans appeared as pure cowboy jeans, differing from the miner image of Levi's and the railway worker image of Lee. Wrangler got its inspiration from the American West spirit and fully displayed the resolute but restrained strength of American Western cowboys. The letter W on the back can also be simultaneously interpreted as work, war and West, symbolising the role of jeans and Wrangler in American history.

Lee Cooper 1908

Lee Cooper was started in London in 1908 and can be called the pioneer of European jeans. It made important contributions to jeans in the 1950s when it introduced design and cut by gender. After Lee's zips, Lee Cooper started the second revolution in female jeans, moving the zips from the side to the front.

Marithé François Girbaud 1964

Famous French brand Marithé François Girbaud, which came to being in 1964, is wildly popular throughout Europe because husband-and-wife team Marithé and François have offered people a totally new concept of wearing jeans with their humanistic approach. Marithé François Girbaud also endowed much more vitality to denim by means of radon technology, environment-friendly dying techniques and a 3D cut that simulates the human body.

Calvin Klein 1968

As jeans become increasingly popular, more and more designers enter the jeans designing industry. Calvin Klein can
be considered one of the most successful ones. Klein, who is
nicknamed "Calvin the Conqueror", established his own company in 1968. Simplicity and sexiness are the hallmarks of
his designs. His designing aesthetic inclines towards a pure,
simple and elegant style, which is modern yet timeless. In
his 35-year career, he has made an impact with his designs
and marketing as well as his sensitivity to trends and talent
for innovation. He popularised men's underwear that focused
on brand and desirability, making many young men eager to
show off the waistband of their Calvin Klein underwear, which
often peeped out of their jeans. Klein also introduced fashionable yet minimalistic knee-length skirts as well as asymmetrical skirts.

The Calvin Klein label carries other related brands like cK
Calvin Klein and Calvin Klein Jeans. From 1978, the name
"Calvin Klein" has been printed on their jeans. The acronym
"cK" is familiar to almost everyone. Elegant and sporty at
times, the clean-cut clothes of Calvin Klein have swept
cities from Bordeaux in France to Bangkok in Thailand. The
sexiness of Calvin Klein has always been fully illustrated in its
ads. But the real revolution came when a Calvin Klein jeans
commercial starring 15-year-old Brooke Shields showed
her posing provocatively in skin-tight jeans, and proclaiming
that nothing came between her and her Calvins. Amidst the
uproar from the public, sales of his jeans climbed and denim
achieved a new level of sexiness.

Calvin Klein Jeans

the calvin bootcut

Diesel 1978

When Renzo Rosso opened his first store opposite the Levi's store, people thought he had gone mad — how could he sell Italian jeans in America, and right opposite the oldest jeans brand?

Today, America is the largest market for Diesel in the world. Rosso did not hesitate to confirm his brand's position in the American jeans industry: "There is no doubt that Diesel has become the most special jeans brand in America. Though our sales are behind those of Levi's, we don't care. I just want us to be a special brand as we are now." Though the brand only came about in 1978, it was the market leader in Europe for three consecutive years in 1995, 1996 and 1997, and shared the American market equally with Levi's. There are now about 300 Diesel stores around the world.

Diesel has been a dynamic brand since the day of its birth. Before he founded Diesel, Rosso had been the royal designer, making clothes for the Italian palace. He then established a company with two of his friends in 1978. He chose "Diesel" as his brand's name as there was an energy crisis all over the world and diesel was the fuel of choice because its ability to start engines was better than petroleum. Rosso wanted his brand to be as popular as diesel was at that time.

Nevertheless, when the first Diesel jeans came out, people were greatly shocked. With "dirty marks" everywhere, the trousers seemed to have been worn for decades. Yet this is exactly what Diesel desires – unique and "destructive damage and filth" which cannot be duplicated. Diesel's procedures were stonewashing after tailoring. To simulate the oily and

dusty marks from manual work, the jeans were stonewashed in red, light grey and olive green liquids. It is due to all the above features that Diesel has won over the market. As Diesel's jeans look more and more worn out, their prices rise higher and higher. A pair of Diesel jeans costs twice as much as a pair of Levi's jeans, but the Diesel fans pay for them with great alacrity.

Budding designers and brands

With the competitive market and the continual demand for jeans, there are always new designers and new brands of jeans that are unique enough to capture a fan base.

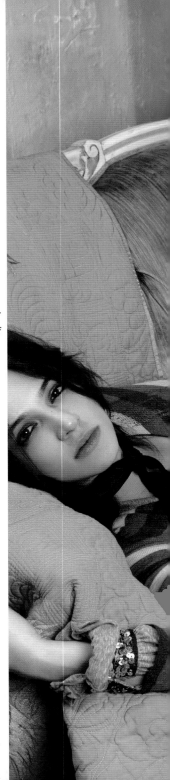

159

Meanwhile, Miss Sixty, an Italian jeans brand, is where many young girls get their perfect pair of sexy jeans. It is Miss Sixty's belief that women should stay tender, charming and sexy, but at the same time, continuously innovate and change their images so that they can make themselves special. And there is Energie, which is one of the top three Italian brands, together with Diesel and Replay. Energie has brought military and retro elements into their design of jeans, making them a great hit all over the world.

There are also smaller niche jeans brands in the market. Acne is one brand that specially designs for models; 5EP is inspired by motorbikers; Fornarina is famous for versatile designing concepts; Earl Jean has the ultimate sexy low-rise jeans; Seven for Mankind is appreciated by Hollywood stars; Joe's jeans have the best fit for hips; and EDWIN, which claims to be representative of Asian jeans, produces the best-shaped denim.

With so many rival brands fighting for a slice of the global jeans pie, competition is tough. Besides perfect technique and quality, a successful jeans brand must also have a unique character as well as a smart marketing strategy.

Penetrating commercials

Good commercials are always able to pinpoint the inner desires of their target audience, tug at their heartstrings and capture their attention. There are excellent commercials for jeans, which are as talked about as the jeans brands themselves.

They all wear Levi's

When cowboys were fervently admired across America, the astute Levi Strauss immediately made use of the trend to advertise its products. In Levi's early illustrated advertisements, there were cowboys on galloping horses on the Western grassland. They all wore Mexican cowboy hats, bright bandannas, knee-high boots and most importantly, Levi's jeans.

When Levi's launched its classic 501 jeans, a very special ad was used to emphasise their uniqueness. Even by today's standards, the ad is still impressive and attractive. There is only a big boxing sandbag hung in the picture. On the right side of the sandbag, there is a red tab – the same tab that is stitched on the right pocket of all Levi's jeans. The tagline reads: "Levi's 501, born wearable." The ad communicates the quality of Levi's 501 jeans: endurable, strong and wearable, no matter how much they are abused.

LEVI'S®

501® JEANS

173

Running on Diesel

What makes the young so crazy about Diesel? Maybe its advertisements can offer an explanation. Since the day it was launched, Diesel has had a definite direction – finding out the attitudes and ideas of the young and designing for them. Rosso once said, "We are not selling products. We are bringing a way of life to everybody." It calls for youths to view the world from different angles and face life with an active and wise attitude. So Diesel's ads are always breaking the mould and imploring the young to always be themselves. It is this detached and unique attitude that wins the youths over.

Diesel's ads are always pushing the envelope

Diesel ads do not have good-looking young men and women posing or any flirty provocation. Their ads go all out to push the envelope. Two sailors kissing passionately. A nun trying hard to tear her habit apart. Diesel ads go against conventions and their audacity is shocking, but their message about individuality is clear. That is what the young like about them.

Nothing comes between me and my Calvins

When Calvin Klein stepped into the jeans industry in the 1970s, he focused on sexy jeans.

His controversial commercials were unforgettable. He chose 15-year-old actress-model Brooke Shields as his ad model. With her hair flying and one hand on her hip, young Shields purred in a sexy voice, "Nothing comes between me and my Calvins." The provocative ad caused a public uproar, and many accused Klein of exploiting child sexuality. But the ad caused a great sales boom. Also, nearly all of Calvin Klein jeans ads are black and white, to convey a simplicity that has become its trademark.

Klein Jeans

Chapter III Superstars and Their Jeans

Good Luck
John Wayne

Denim jeans have absorbed some of the star power from popular celebrities, who are seen wearing jeans in their movies and in their everyday lives. As a result, jeans became more and more popular as regular people on the street started donning jeans to look more like their favourite movie stars.

Marilyn Monroe

The Duke – John Wayne

John Wayne, "the Duke", is well-known for his cowboy heroism in his films. Since he first entered the movie industry, he
was always cast as righteous men upholding justice and the
law. The film *Stagecoach* in 1939 shot him to fame. He played
a series of tough, aggressive, brave and firm cowboys from
the American West, who rode horses and handled guns with
ease. He was considered a hero by Americans.

Good Luck John Wayne

Cowboy hero in the making: the young John Wayne

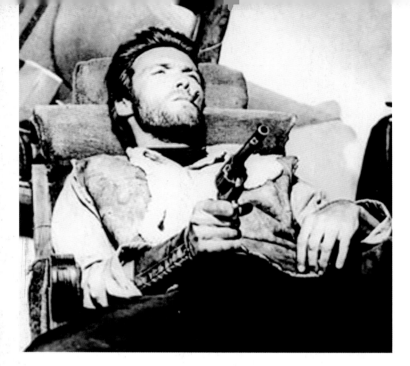

Old cowboy – Clint Eastwood

Clint Eastwood was a very popular star in the late 1960s. Wearing capes, jeans and holding a cigar between his teeth, his image in *A Fistful of Dollars* was worshipped throughout America and Europe. He was forever a cowboy to his fans. But ironically, he is allergic to horses. Eastwood has proven his mettle in the uncertain industry – he is one of the rare few who have taken the roles of actor, director and producer in Hollywood. In 2000, when he was already 70 years old, the old cowboy was still passionate and strong enough to make the film *Space Cowboys* with colleagues who were similarly devoted to their craft.

Nature boy – James Dean

When it came to showing personality through jeans, James Dean was unquestionably the star who could do it best. In the 1950s, those who wore jeans were called "nature boys" and James Dean was the most typical prototype. His role in the movie *Rebel Without a Cause* in 1955 made young men want to follow his style. Some say that Marlon Brando changed the way people behaved, while James Dean changed the way people lived their lives. Stuart Stein, the screenwriter of *Rebel Without a Cause* recalled, "People dressed in the way he dressed himself, and people walked in the way he walked." In his personal life, Dean often wore Levi's jeans with holes and a white T-shirt. He didn't shave, didn't comb his hair, and always carried a Zippo lighter. His indifferent attitude towards the outside world and his casual lifestyle was eagerly imitated by rebellious youngsters. Jeans thus became their "uniform".

JAMES DEAN® THE ORIGIN 50th Anniversary

196

The wild one – Marlon Brando

Besides James Dean, Marlon Brando was also one of the popular "nature boys". In 1951's *A Streetcar Named Desire*, his costume was simply a pair of tight blue jeans and a dirty wet white T-shirt, which brought out his natural, impulsive and uncontrollable personality in the film. In his 1953 film, *The Wild One*, Marlon Brando wore bleached jeans, showing his tough and handsome side, not to mention his manly aura which differed from Dean's nonchalance. In his pair of jeans, Brando was bursting with charm.

The sex goddess – Marilyn Monroe

Marilyn Monroe was the first to inject sexiness into jeans for women. In her films in the 1950s, she appeared in blue jeans often. With her curvy figure coupled with her enigmatic almond eyes and flaming-red lips, she oozed sex appeal and got the nickname "blonde bombshell". In a scene in *The Misfits*, the camera zoomed in on her hips, wrapped snugly in blue jeans, while she was riding a horse. People generally agree that Marilyn Monroe was synonymous with sexiness. Her natural body language together with her blue jeans made for a sexy but sweet picture.

The blonde bombshell: Marilyn Monroe

Marilyn Monroe

Marilyn Monroe

Jennifer Lopez

Britney Spears

Popular stars are undoubtedly the perfect image representatives for jeans. Their unique personalities also give their jeans different flavours. In the music video, *Don't Tell Me*, Dsquared2 jeans, together with Madonna's sharp and haunting eyes and her toned body, perfectly showcased her wild and attractive features. For Jennifer Lopez, her famous derriere is given a bigger lift when she puts her jeans on. Britney Spears, on the other hand, became recognised for her sex appeal when she ditched her sweet schoolgirl attire for cropped tops and low-rise jeans. In fact, Spears has been credited for popularising low-rise jeans.

Jennifer Lopez

Avril Lavigne

Avril Lavigne

Chapter IV Versatile Jeans

The wonderful thing about jeans is that they can match and fit any figure. Over the last century, their identity has been changing from time to time. Just as they are common and inconspicuous, they can also bring a certain uniqueness that belongs only to the wearer.

If not for the American cowboys, jeans would have been less charming. The American West is a symbol for freedom and adventure. The "horseback heroes" were a group of brave, hardworking and entrepreneurial people. It is this spirit that underlines the appeal of jeans.

219

ALONG the NAVAJO TRAIL
A RE-RELEASE
A REPUBLIC PICTURE

COUNTRY OF ORIGIN U. S. A

ROY ROGERS . TRIGGER
KING OF THE COWBOYS   THE SMARTEST HORSE IN THE MOVIES

R54-162

Western movies were popular throughout the 1930s and 1940s. The handsome and brave cowboys played by the likes of Roy Rogers and John Wayne were deeply rooted in the hearts of the audience. They galloped freely on their horses across the barren desert, wearing broad-rimmed Mexican hats and a Colt revolver at their waist or Winchester rifle on their shoulder, with their ammunition belts slung across their torsos and high leather boots with spurs. Leather jackets, jeans and a bright bandanna also accompanied them on their fleeting journey across the vast deserts. In many literary works, TV programmes and films, Western cowboys appeared as typical representatives of the American spirit of individuality and independence, adventurousness and freedom. Closely related to the cowboy's life, blue jeans were also associated with such values.

The righteous and handsome "King of Cowboys", Roy Rogers

A painting by English artist Graham Leggett, who specialises in Western portraits

Of course, the real cowboys could not be defending justice all day long. In reality, they were busy earning a living. Cowboys usually looked after ranch cows, which was a hard and time-consuming job with little pay. During the winter, they had to look for other jobs to make ends meet. Due to the rapid increase in demand for beef from 1865 to 1895 in America, ranch owners in the South-west raised many cows and then transported them to the markets in the East using the railway networks. The job of the cowboys was to feed the cows in the open and then drive them to the nearest railway station.

Young people at the rodeo dance during the Arizona Cowpunchers Reunion Rodeo, the largest amateur rodeo in Arizona. Only working ranch cowboys and their families can participate in the rodeo – professional rodeo cowboys are not allowed to

RIBBON
ROPERS

STEER
RIDERS

In the harsh outdoor conditions, cowboy hats, jeans and high boots became their trusted companions. Cowboy hats could protect them from wind and rain; multi-pocketed jeans allowed them to bring enough daily necessities; the warm, waterproof and comfortable high boots were also a must since they travelled constantly. The bandanna was also extremely useful as a dust mask, a neck covering to protect the cowboy from the sun, a handkerchief, an ear covering in cold weather, a signal flag, a water strainer, or even a tourniquet if needed. When a cowboy passed away, their faces would be covered by a bandanna, a symbol of their life and a companion to ensure their tranquil comfort in death.

The tough and tenacious cowboys, who were at the base of the social ladder, became the pioneers of the Western movement. Likewise, jeans, which were their work-wear, became associated with their rough-it-out attitude, heroism and their sense of adventure.

Not only that, jeans became the symbol of Americanism as seen from the Hollywood movies in the early 20th century.

In *The Skyscrapers of New York*, shot in 1906, workers in jeans were doing brickwork high above the city or soldering metal parts while balancing on the scaffolding. Skyscrapers, chimneys and scaffolding made up the scenery in the movie. The workers in jeans and the New York skyline were the leading characters of this movie.

In *The Girl at the Cupola*, shot in 1912, the protagonist was a common worker in jeans and managed to resolve a conflict with the workers. Hence, jeans also fitted a democratic and just character.

Jeans and jeans wear imbued a sense of American historic reality in these early movies. At the same time, an "American" character also started to develop in jeans as a result of these movies.

American children imitating the look and stance of cowboys

Shrink to fit. Button fly. Now cut for women.

50

LEVI'S
WOMENSW...

This association was further strengthened during the two World Wars, when jeans were ordered to be military uniforms by the government. Women military workers were often seen in loose working jeans wear with rolled-up sleeves and trousers, powerful arms and steady gazes reflecting their willingness to serve their country. As such, it became more acceptable and common for women to wear jeans even during the post-war period.

During the Great Depression between the two World Wars, people were facing unemployment, poverty and starvation. The US started a comprehensive photographing plan that aimed to record the progress of the newly implemented economic policy in the form of photos. Farm owners, farmers and immigrants were all photographed wearing jeans work-wear. It was a good bargain because the jeans were handed out as part of a welfare package for uniforms in some places, and at the same time, these jeans were photographed as a symbol of the US. In the mid-1930s, even notices and ads all made use of people in jeans to express American issues because in their eyes, jeans wear and Americans could not be separated.

le CD N°1
de la disc
idéale du

Pour seulement

Ego, rebellion and anti-tradition

The first example of jeans as a symbol of "anti-tradition" appeared in the artist immigrant district in Santa Fe after the wars. These artists objected to capitalism, consumerism, corruption and discrimination, and took to wearing jeans as a team symbol. Jeans meant freedom and equality and the group used it as a utopian symbol of democracy and anti-corruption.

245

A modern American family in jeans

Meanwhile, the rebellious character of jeans also permeated rock music. Bill Haley recorded a group of rock songs with his band Bill Haley and His Comets, all in jeans. The king of rock 'n' roll, Elvis Presley, wore metal-riveted jeans and T-shirts. His sexy voice, wry smile, dance moves and big sideburns were a hit with the young.

Rock singers immediately realised the rebellious streak in jeans. They capitalised on it, behaving unconventionally and unorthodoxly with the help of jeans to convey their dissatisfaction with society.

Gene Vincent doodled his most famous work, *Be-Bop-A-Lula,* on his jeans and jacket. His fans followed his lead and decorated their clothes with military elements: edging, studs, metal buttons and national tab designs were all over their jeans and T-shirts. Even skull shapes and swastikas were put on the jeans and jackets. When the famous rock concert promoter Bill Graham was publicising his music on the American West Coast, his jeans and black T-shirt helped him gel with the fans. Also, Jimi Hendrix, David Crosby, Stephen Stills, Graham Nash and Neil Young turned their jeans into glaring rebel symbols while conveying their ideals through their rock music. The flared jeans that The Beatles wore were glamorous and popular, but they also gave the superstar band some common ground with their fans.

Elvis Presley

The Beatles – John Lennon, Paul McCartney, George Harrison, Ringo Starr

John Lennon

When pop art proclaimed that art should not be aristocratic and should be attached to reality, there was instant agreement from the masses. As this trend spread from the UK to the US, one of the most immediate responses to it appeared in the form of jeans which broke the fashion norms at that time. Marilyn Monroe's smiling face was printed on jeans, and so were portraits of Madonna. Chloé used musician's faces as design decorations on jeans. More and more jeans were designed with patterns of soda bottles and movie stars. Popular elements were dots, sexy and exaggerated red lips and classic black-and-white stripes.

The punk culture grew quickly in London in the 1970s, and it soon discovered jeans for its extremeness, decadence and rebel spirit. The result of the merger produced exaggerated metal buttons and paillettes, which were all over jeans jackets. Tears, holes, and raw edges were also the norm. Designer Vivienne Westwood, often cited as the creator of punk, did numerous "tricks" on jeans wear, such as tearing collars, sewing beads on the fabric, buckling pins, adding zips or doodling on the cloth, and combining denim with materials like leather or plastic.

Their unique and special rebellious traits guarantee that punk jeans are still able to influence the fashion world today. Doodled pictures and colourful graffiti in pop art style are also found on jeans now. Levi's, in a bid to combine fashion and street art, co-operated with famous American artist Slick, and 11 artists such as Green and Kofie and Cat, in a way that overthrew tradition. They doodled, in a very hip-hop style, on different stonewashed denim jeans jackets. The result was 12 unique, manually-stretched jeans jackets.

Energie's jeans designs are influenced by punk culture and pop art

Miss Sixty strives to make women look special with their innovative jeans designs

Superior customisation

As early as the 1960s, Henry Duarte began to tailor-make jeans. Some of his clients included rock 'n' roll stars like Steven Tyler, Lenny Kravitz and Jon Bon Jovi, who popularised super low-rise tight-fitting jeans that were like a second skin. Decorated in frosted glass, Duarte's workshop at Melrose Street in Los Angeles is extremely exclusive. It only receives appointed customers – regular walk-in customers will not be served. Celebrities such as Gwyneth Paltrow, Nicole Kidman and Madonna are frequent patrons, but even they have to wait patiently for over a month to get their jeans customised.

The super low-rise tight-fitting jeans style designed by Henry Duarte was a hit with rock stars like Steven Tyler of Aerosmith

Celebrities usually get their jeans tailor-made

With fertile imagination and creativity by both designer and client, a pair of jeans can become a piece of art. But this comes at a price. APO Jeans now offers customised 24-carat platinum and diamond buttons on its jeans at a price of US$4,000. Escada's customised jeans typically start at US$7,500, its most expensive pair being the Escada Couture Swarovski Crystal jeans which cost US$10,000. For that pair, the entire side of the jeans is encrusted in a waterfall of Swarovski crystals.

While the style of the jeans, such as straight or boot-cut, is relatively standard, the decorations that adorn them are infinitely variable. Such customised designs can be expensive, but they are still fervently pursued by fashionistas who want to stand out.

Besides having retail shops, Gap also tailor makes jeans for VIPs

Extravagant customisations include Swarovski crystals being encrusted on the entire side of jeans

The three-dimensional Miss Sixty emblem

Miss Sixty's popular skinny jeans

"Do you see any paparazzi out here?" came the doorman's reply. There were none.

Miss Barton's concerns might have been a tad presumptuous. No one seemed to recognize the sultry "O.C." star.

"Mischa Barton? Who is that?" asked a non-TV watcher at the club. "I just said hi to Brandon, but who's Mischa?"

Nevertheless, the starlet hid her face and physically attached herself to Davis as they were escorted through the packed club to the private VIP room.

But this diva-in-training episode was a rerun. At a recent private party, she snapped when two girls asked who she was, Barton hissed. "You just hate me because I'm famous!" Maybe.

SUSAN WHO?

Feisty, beautiful redheads obviously do it for **Tim Robbins**. And there he was engaged in what one could only assume was an erudite political conversation with one last Thursday. But it was 2 a.m. and her name definitely wasn't **Susan Sarandon**.

After the 46-year-old actor showed up at Bungalow 8 in the wee hours with his much shorter pal **Sean Penn**, the two occupied a corner table where they were immediately surrounded by enthusiastic clubgoers.

The model-tall, flame-haired woman quickly engrossed Robbins in a gabfest. And the oh-so serious twosome were at it into the wee hours. After an hour standing with their heads together by one of the potted palm trees that decorate the club, the two took a seat at a secluded table.

They didn't even come up for air when Penn finally took his leave at 2:30 a.m., glad-handing fans on his way out the door. Back at the table, Robbins moved in a little closer. Dead man walking?

MISCHA BARTON: Desperately in need of more paparazzi to avoid.

Sara Jaye/Abaca

THE SONG IS OVER

Man your texting cellphones, The perfect downtown couple a DJ **Mark Ronson** and his actres **Rashida Jones**, have called it q more than a year of engagem

For Jones, who used movie star **Tobey M.** this is the second tim heart's been broken. former duo, who had common impeccabl pedigrees, were a c and popular fixture parties across the c Jones, the 27-year-Harvard-educated of **Peggy Lipton** **Quincy Jones**, a Ronson, the 2 stepson of For **Mick Jones**, two years befo proposed — by customizing a crossword puz read "Will you mer?"

But last Frid Ronson was s opening night Ruby Falls in — and enterta crowd of ski dressed chick his spinning

STILL JEN BOY 'TROY

Brad Pitt Jennifer A were maki like a coup teenagers Bungalow Monday n The pair fl packed "Troy party at Ciprian Street, and anyo actually spoke to disarmingly flirt Pitt was immedia tackled by teenage asking frantically. nice? Is he nice?"

The couple, clear prom king and quee celeb world, with th impossibly shiny hai perfectly even tans a alarmingly white smil a hasty retreat out th entrance and headed f Bungalow 8, where **Bo** already taken up reside back table to celebrate h birthday.

Among famous friends superagent **Bryan Lour** supermodels **Cindy Cr** and **Helena Christens** and Aniston — still the ooking pair in the roo made out right at the ta "They looked very m couple," said one clubg "They were having a go time." What a skirt chas

Pop stars in Miss Sixty jeans

As mass market jeans become increasingly common, people start moving towards tailor-made jeans in order to be unique

Creating individuality

Unfortunately, most people are unable to afford such exorbitant customisations. Ordinary jeans brands are also unable to provide such services at a low cost because they are usually small outfits that lack advanced processing techniques.

But with the help of the Internet, relatively cheaper customisation is readily available to more people.

Currently, customers of IC3D (Interactive Custom Clothes Company) and UJeans can design and order their jeans through their websites. For example, IC3D uses modular designing techniques to customise jeans. The jeans are divided into 11 modules – gender, fabric, fit, leg, ankle, waist, front, back, fly, details and thread – with different options for each module to choose from. When the customers have decided on the 11 modules, they can input their size and complete the order. Then the work is transferred to the production line and the pair of customised jeans can be created.

UJeans is another company that offers this service. They have more than 33,000 different styles of jeans to ensure that customers can design the jeans to suit their tastes. Their jeans are made to fit using 11 body measurements of the customer, and take about five to seven weeks to produce.

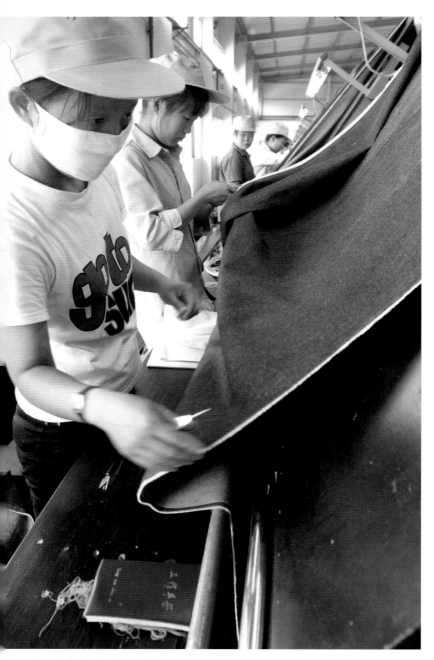

A denim factory in Canton, China

Rock-washed jeans from Energie are popular among the stars

Stitched patterns are common customisations for jeans

289

Levi's provides customers with thousands of styles and colours of jeans

Levi's has thousands of jeans of different styles and colours, but even so, customers who want the best possible fit can pay US$10 more to get their jeans customised. The jeans will take a fortnight to produce. The move towards customisation has proved so popular that the company's turnover has tripled after introducing it.

This goes to show that for customers who want perfectly fitting jeans, customisation is worth the wait and the price.

Chapter VI Styles of Jeans

The evolution of different styles of jeans – from the use of different materials to the complexity of its decorations, and even to the return and adaptation of old styles of jeans – is a creative force that brings much joy to fans.

A wide variety

They may be so low they can barely cover the hip, or so long that they have to be rolled up. They may be thin like a matchstick, or so wide they can fit two legs. They can be simply washed in pure blue, or adorned with garish ornaments. The styles of jeans are diverse and are constantly being altered according to trends and tastes.

Everyone has their favourite pair

Overalls were the earliest style of jeans. They were originally worn by men, but when they were in fashion, it was the women who snapped them up. They felt that the comfort as well as the masculine style of the overalls made them look and feel more suave and confident. In large overalls, the delicate figure of a woman can be casually and subtly shown.

301

Basically, overalls were designed either with tight or broad trousers. They were usually one-piece, with a slightly tight hip, broad legs and wide laces near the feet. Some people feel that overalls look foolishly simple, yet others may find some overalls garish with their big pockets, bowknots or embroidered patterns.

Women were big fans of overalls when they were in fashion

When it comes to an enduring traditional style of jeans, look no further than straight jeans. Straight jeans are cut straight down from the thigh, with the wearer's hips being the only "bump" in the jeans. This cut is suitable for both shapely and plump people as it makes their legs look lankier. With the improvement of craftsmanship, jeans of some brands have been cut straighter than their original style. The bottom end of straight jeans can also be cuffed. With these modifications, straight jeans can be regarded as the most classic and simple, yet most lively and unique style.

The popularity of other styles of jeans, however, depends on personal tastes and fashion trends.

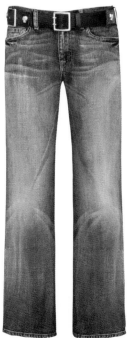

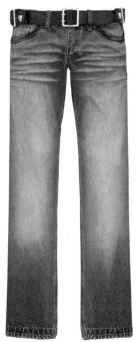

Loose straight jeans are a variation of straight jeans. They are only slightly "collapsed", unlike baggy "hip-hop" jeans. In recent years, loose straight jeans have become very fashionable in South Korea.

One of the most exaggerated styles of jeans is baggy "hip-hop" jeans that are a product of hip-hop culture. This "collapsed" style is worn low, and makes it hard to see any body contours or proportions below the waist. Hip-hoppers are proud of their baggy jeans, and the jeans are in turn used as a symbol of hip-hop. Even though the brands may not be well-known outside their sub-culture, these jeans are still well-liked by people who are into hip-hop.

313

Boot-cut jeans are those that have a little flare at the ends. The upper part of the jeans leg is slightly narrow, and the lower part below the knees is slightly wider. This makes them more able to mould themselves to the wearer's figure due to their unique clipping style, which shapes a line from the knee to the slightly flared bottom. This makes the calves look longer and creates the illusion that the wearer has become taller and thinner. Large flared jeans, once very popular in the 1970s, are also liked by some people today. Hippie flares that are skin-tight and have ripped holes in their trouser legs are also still seen.

Slight boot-cut flares such as Levi's 517 are usually worn by youngsters. Other slim-cut jeans like Levi's 606 also make the legs more elongated and sexy. Jeans styles that are above the knee are also popular during spring and summer seasons. But when it comes to sexiness today, low-rise jeans take the biscuit. The waistband of the jeans clings tightly to the hip bone, showing off the wearer's figure. In fact, the waists of jeans are becoming lower and the rise – the distance between the crotch and the waist – shorter. Celebrities like Britney Spears and Jennifer Lopez have also popularised this trend by exuding sex appeal in their low-rise jeans. Frankie B's "dangerously low" jeans, which have a very low rise of three inches, unapologetically show off much hip. Now, with the addition of Lycra, low-rise jeans can be tighter and stretchier, pushing up the hips and making the fabric around the legs tauter.

Whether long or short, skinny or baggy, jeans almost never lose their appeal with the masses.

Magnificent decorations

When it comes to decorating the jeans, all designers are consummate masters in various crafts such as embroidering, collaging, beading, fringing, printing, perforating and piecing together flannelette, fur, percale, leather, silk cloth and denim cloth. For example, they may rivet a row of punk-style studs along the pocket, or stitch gorgeous crystal beads onto drainpipe trousers, or encrust the whole trouser flank with Swarovski crystals.

Embroidery, a craft which has a history of over 3,000 years, acquires a new life when used to decorate jeans. With the introduction of light jeans fabric, many embroidery designs that were previously confined to cotton and yarn can now be sewn on jeans as well. Various designs of rare flowers and grasses, birds and animals as well as minority totems have all been used to decorate jeans.

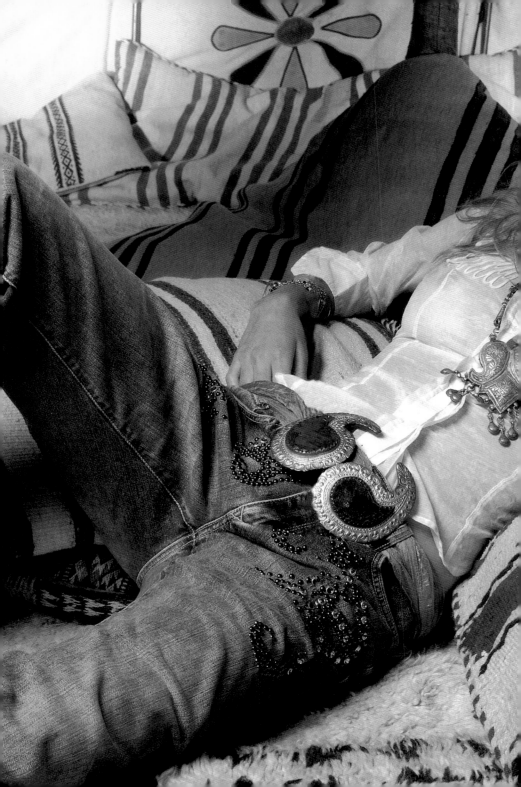

For example, Brazilian label Iódice has a pair of jeans with a wool-embroidered three-dimensional picture of a tropical jungle. French fashion house Chloé has also made use of embroidery on its jeans. Its subtle designs near the hip, such as a red flower set off by the blue of the jeans pocket, or a pair of flying wings embroidered on both sides of the whitened back pockets, all add some character to their jeans.

Alternatively, designs can be printed on jeans. Some, like Baroque-style totems, Mexican flowers and Japanese cartoons, have been printed to add an exotic flavour to American jeans.

Another form of embellishment is the addition of decorative fringes on jeans. They could be colourful beads, clipped jeans cloth, silk or leather-like braids – these fringes give a carefree gypsy feel to a pair of jeans. Ripped jeans also create such an effect. The blue façade of jeans is because of the blue-coloured warp, which are the lengthwise threads, and the white ripped frays are due to the white-coloured weft, which are crosswise threads. Hence, with skilful ripping and fraying, the jeans can have tasteful "borders" of white cloth at ripped sections, or have a drooping and unruly effect from the white-coloured frays. This is unique to denim cloth as its fabric is solid and thick and does not disintegrate when torn.

Collage, a craft favoured by avant-garde dressmakers, is also used on jeans now. Logos, badges and motifs can all be used in a collage on jeans, a style that is rather reminiscent of pop art. Apart from collaging with denim cloths of different colours, it is also possible, and in fact increasingly common, to collage with fur, velour, corduroy or leather. Dior has designed a kind of water-washed blue leather-collaged jeans, with one half being denim cloth and the other half being leather. Brazil-born New York fashion designer Carlos Miele prefers collaging with soft materials like velour, chiffon and silk as softer materials add a dynamic flow to the strength and firmness of denim.

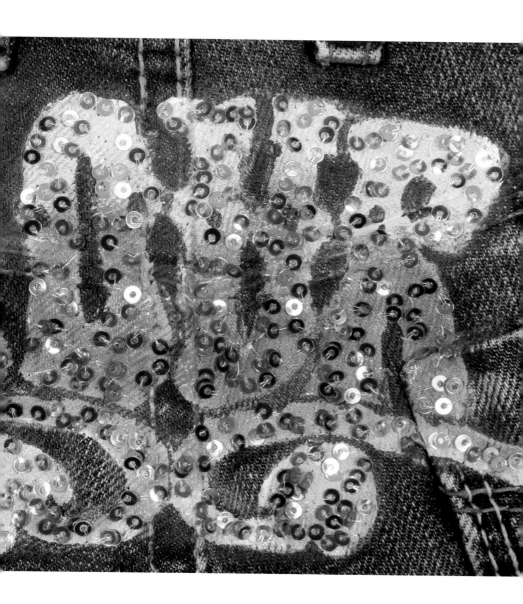

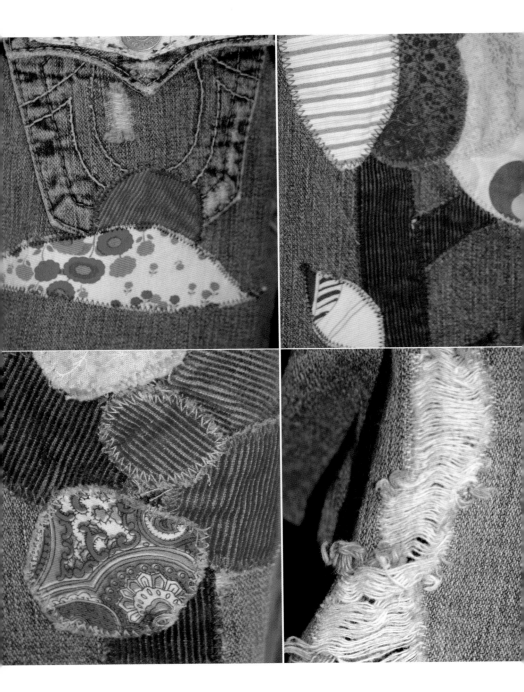

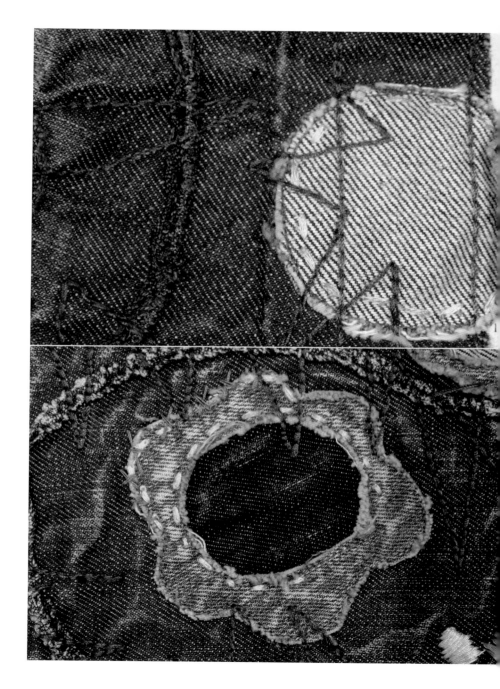

The most popular processing method revolves around whitening, for example Levi's and XFinish's archaised colourwashing, Wry Finish's artificial trace left by brushing, Bobson's blitz-like whitened lines, which are called "ghost claws", and Wrangler's deep water-washing. After whitening, the denim are usually tinted in colours of different hues, such as yellow, green or light blue, natural verdigris green and soil brown.

There is also the popular Japanese "crush" processing method, introduced by labels like Sweet Camel, which combines paint-staining and aperture-boring. Such jeans look like the designer has carelessly spilled dye on the jeans cloth, or the wearer has splattered mud all over themselves. There are also "mouldy" jeans, which are washed, blanched and dyed to look like they are mouldy. In fact, Diesel has developed a "Flow Dye" or "Drift Ice Dye" style, which involves bleaching the black denim damask three times, and then pouring cold dyestuff to form colours such as grey, blue, black and white, to make the jeans look worn out and mouldy.

Apart from creating unconventional effects by special methods of processing the fabric, jeans designers also pay attention to increasing the benefits of wearing their jeans. For example, Texwood's latest series of light jeans has CoolMax by DuPont added to its fabric. CoolMax supposedly moves moisture away from the body and allows the fabric to dry faster, leaving the wearer cool at all times. Anti-bacterial material is also used in some jeans fabric to prevent body odours. Other practical additions are anti-wrinkle, anti-dirt and even anti-static jeans. But probably the most "healthy" of all are Brappers jeans which contain collagen to tighten the skin, as well as elements to hydrate and nourish the skin with Vitamin C. On top of the various functions of these jeans, their materials still feel soft, smooth and comfortable to put on.

The big Levi's jeans display in Shanghai's Xu Jia Hui commercial centre attracts much attention

Package deal

Jeans designers will not pass up any chance to let their imagination and creativity take over. Their pursuit of quality and design also means that any part of a pair of jeans, whether it is the pockets, trouser legs or decorations, is well designed.

335

Pockets

Originally used for storing things, pockets nowadays are now also serving an aesthetic function. Pockets come in many designs today: asymmetrical, three-dimensional, pleated and multi-pockets, just to name a few. Apart from modifying the shape and position of pockets, designers also decorate them with studs, jewels, Swarovski crystals, prints and embroidered patterns.

When Levi's produced its first 501 jeans, it was likely that they never imagined that the design on their back pockets would be used as a blueprint for many manufacturers, who improvised on the trademark double arc and red tab. Italian label Fornarina, which has jeans that are famous for enhancing the hips, also puts in much effort to decorate its jeans pockets. Some designs that it has introduced on the back pockets are riveted diamonds or studs, pinned up iron patches and even long metal chains inspired by hip-hop style.

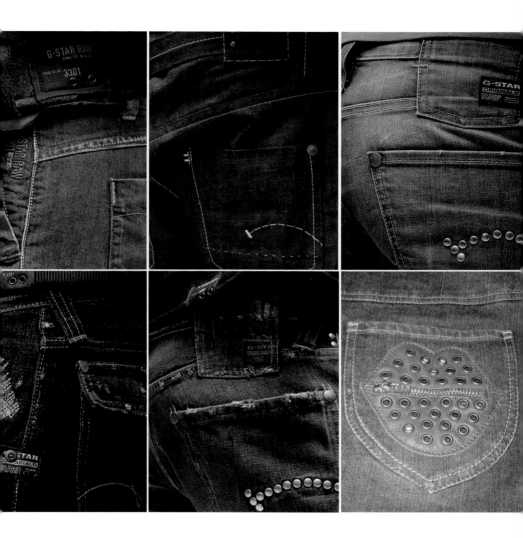

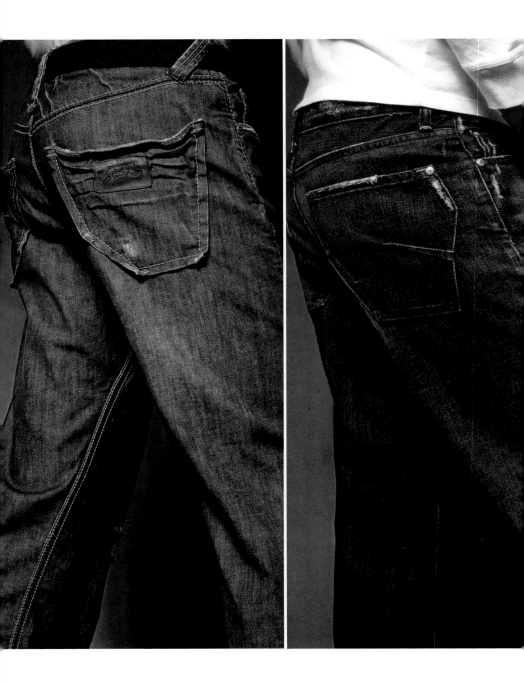

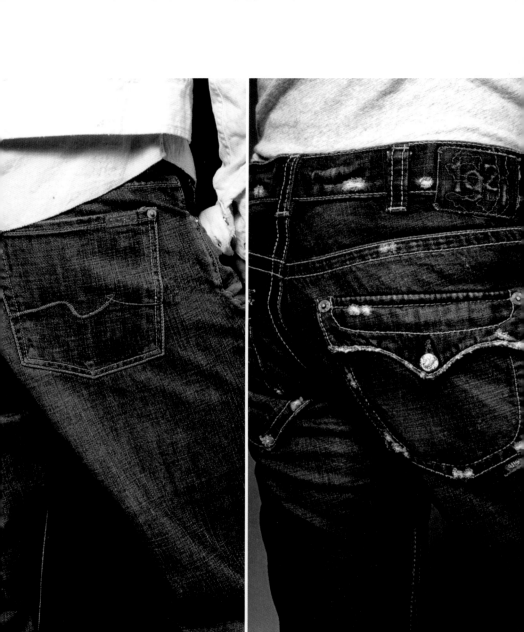

Stitch-setting

Apart from assembling pieces of cloth together, stitches also serve to decorate as well as create certain visual effects. For example, the stitches on the back pockets can make the hip look much smaller. By manipulating the texture, colour, thickness and position of these stitch-settings, a whole variety of different looks can be achieved for the pair of jeans.

Set on denim

Denim is not only about jeans. The popularity of denim and jeans has spawned many other jeans-related accessories and apparel such as hats, skirts, jackets, bags and so on. Each of them comes in a wide variety of styles and has its own unique characteristics.

OWN A PIECE OF HISTORY

BROKEBACK
MOUNTAIN
AUCTION

THE ENTIRE WARDROBE FROM THIS GROUND
BREAKING FILM INCLUDING ITEMS WORN BY
ACTORS JAKE GYLLENHAAL AND HEATH LEDGER

OCTOBER 13TH TO 20TH

COWBOY HATS, BOOTS, JEANS AND MORE
LETTER OF AUTHENTICITY INCLUDED WITH EACH SALE

CELEBRATE THE IMPACT OF THIS HISTORICAL FILM
BY BIDDING ON THESE ONE OF A KIND ITEMS AT WWW.SEENON.COM

PROCEEDS FROM THE SALE OF THESE UNIQUE ITEMS TO BENEFIT HRC
©2006 ALL RIGHTS RESERVED. SEENON!™ IS A REGISTERED TRADEMARK OF DELIVERY AGENT,INC.

HUMAN
RIGHTS
CAMPAIGN®

FOCUS
FEATURES

Jeans jackets

Jeans jackets are almost on par with leather jackets in achieving the cool, punk look. Some jackets have multiple zips on their sleeves, making them look like biker jackets. Others made of old stonewashed denim exude a vintage style. When cut in the style of suit jackets, the denim and wash of jeans jackets also manage to inject some casual chic into the otherwise serious design. But the most popular designs now are cropped jeans jackets for women. They convey a kind of trendy youthfulness and can be matched with anything from short skirts to long trousers.

Jeans skirts

Miniskirts are still the most popular style when it comes to jeans skirts, even though to look good in them, women have to have an excellent figure. Whether they are thrown together with a loose coat and a pair of boots, matched with a sports jacket, or worn ripped and frayed, the jeans miniskirt brings with it a grungy kind of sexiness.

355

Jeans hats

Jeans hats sometimes take a Western style, with matching copper widgets and beautiful feathers at times. Designers have created many new jeans hats that do not only cater to those who want a Western rodeo look. These include sports-utility hats, duckbill hats, fisherman's hats and piquant berets in colours such as blue, green and black.

Jeans bags

The durability and trendiness of denim also make it a good material for bags. These casual bags range from totes and shoulder-slings to rucksacks. Even brands like Miu Miu and Louis Vuitton have made jeans bags a part of their collections.

The future of denim

Designers have racked their brains to expand the scope of jeans products. Jean Paul Gaultier has even used denim to make dresses, including evening dresses, to show that the popular but casual fabric can also be made elegant. Even denim bikinis and underwear have shown up on the market. With the advancement of processing and production methods, it will probably come as no surprise if more and more jeans products appear in the future.

Denim DIY

Instead of discarding their old jeans, some people modify them into dresses, skirts and even cushions. Old jeans can also be converted to jeans accessories like bags, waistbands, bandanas or jeans straps decorated with paillettes. Those who have grown tired of their denim miniskirts can add a laced petticoat underneath to create a longer, more feminine skirt. Last season's jeans can also be tweaked by tearing the edges, embroidering patterns or adding beads and crystals. Some even add feathers, lace or knotted wool to the sides and corners of their jeans to make them more unique.

Designers preparing to modify jeans

Another form of DIY that is done by jeans fans is to change a brand-new pair of jeans into a classic pair of "old" jeans. These hardcore fans only buy brand new jeans that do not have faded colours, and spend three to five years "creating" their own pair of jeans from that pair. To make the colour of the jeans fade naturally, they try their best to wear their jeans all the time and wash them as rarely as possible, as water and detergent may make the colours fade more quickly, re-sulting in an unnatural fade. In order to achieve this effect, they need to have immense patience to tolerate the dirt, smell and stares from passersby. They also must have the proper sitting and standing posture in order for the jeans to develop

A DIY denim skirt

the right whiskers. Whiskers are the white creases around the crotch and knee areas that are usually bleached or applied. Not all jeans will be able to achieve this "devolution" – it depends on their material, dyes and decorations, to name but a few factors. For these fans, only those jeans that stick to the classic form are worth their time and effort. And a classic pair of jeans is one with no less than ten working procedures in its manufacture, as this allows it to keep its original elasticity and shape forever.

Passersby enthralled by a huge artwork of jeans on display

**Chapter VII Crazy Over Jeans:
Alex, Jeans Collector from Hong Kong**

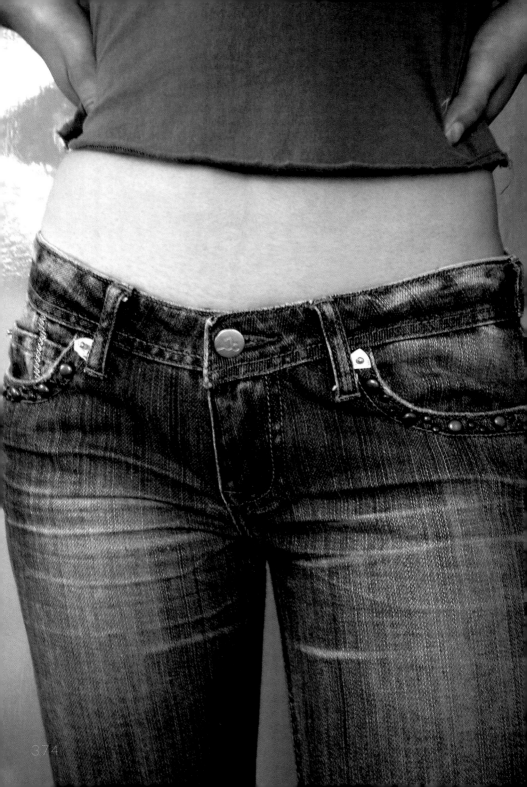

374

Tell us about yourself.

I grew up in Vancouver and came back to study in Hong Kong.

Tell us about the first pair of jeans that you collected.

The first pair I collected is the 1972 Levi's 501, which I got from my friend's father. It was originally used in a creativity contest, so there's a lot of graffiti on it. Up to today, it has never been worn. At the beginning, I didn't collect on a serious basis. But after buying more and more pairs of jeans, I suddenly realised that there were 40 to 50 pairs in my wardrobe, and that I would naturally chat with my friends over the Internet to find out or exchange information about jeans. Now I've collected over 200 pairs of jeans.

If I travel to Thailand, I spend one or two days searching for special jeans in the Bangkok second-hand market, where I might find a pair of Levi's 501XX from 1944. Some magazines approached me to write about jeans collecting, so I started writing for some fashion magazines to share my experiences with readers.

What are the main brands that you usually collect?

There are so many. I have collected some Levi's 501XX classic styles, like the 501 series with Levi's printed in all-capital letters on its logo. This series was manufactured between 1939 and 1969, but after 1970, this was changed to small letters except for the 'L', which makes its collection value much lower. I have also collected many current styles of LVC in limited editions. The rest I have collected are mainly Japanese labels like Evisu, NBHD and Sugar Cane, as well as Energie and G-Star. Besides those, I have also collected two pairs of Versace jeans, which really had whopping price tags. Actually I prefer to collect jeans with special craftwork or those that are limited editions. Also, I collect original versions of second-hand jeans, which are rarely found these days.

When it comes to Japanese jeans, like Evisu, Neighborhood, EDWIN, and in recent years, A Bathing Ape, which do you think is the best?

All of them are good. I don't want to offend any one of them. Haha! Evisu is the post-modern version of Levi's. Its NO.1 series is the one that is most worth collecting, because not every brand can afford the expensive handmade denim cloth. Also, it is manufactured in small numbers. NBHD is rather obscure, so many people don't know it except the true jeans "connoisseurs". Nevertheless, there are many collectors of this brand. Max Savage, the 2003 version of NBHD that Hong Kong actor Edison Chen is a fan of, sold at a price of HKD 9,999. Its 2004 versions, Ripper and Metal, and its 2005 versions, Crack, Lighting and Fragment, are all quite sought after. As for EDWIN, its 503/505 series is the most popular. After Brad Pitt became their spokesman, the 503 series came up with a limited rebel vintage version where every piece of metal on the jeans was pure silver. As for Nigo's A Bathing Ape, I prefer their T-shirts actually. Currently there is also Sugar Cane from Japan, which at first imitated Levi's 501. Its fabric was made by antique-craft machines, and the 1955 and 1966 versions were made in the original Levi's 555 factory. On top of that, these two versions have used 300 zips that remained from the Gripper Zipper factory which has closed down. Therefore, they are very valuable to collectors.

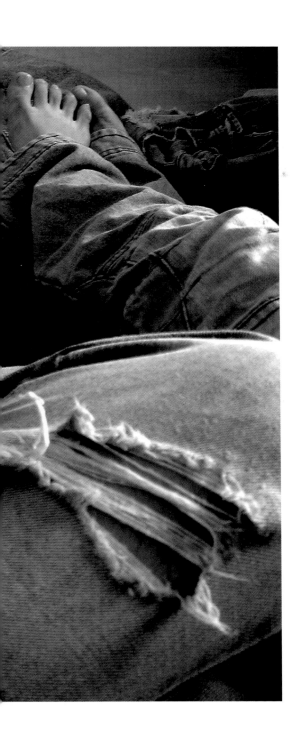

How can you keep the jeans you wear well?

Some of the jeans I've collected are brand-new, some classic styles are second-hand, and others I keep for regular wear. Keeping the jeans you wear well takes time and patience. To mention Evisu NO.1 again, the fabrics it uses are handmade denim cloth, which shrinks a lot after the first washing, but makes the jeans fit better. This kind of jeans is not difficult to shape well. NO.2, on the other hand, may take a longer time to shape as they use fabrics woven by machines. Sugar Cane is also easily maintained in a good condition.

The first wash is very important for jeans. When you buy a pair of jeans, put it in clear water for three hours to remove the starch in it. Sometimes you can put some white vinegar or salt in to make the colour stay as much as possible, but never put it in hot water or it will shrink excessively. Afterwards, wash and dry it. It is not advisable to wash your jeans often. Even if you wear the same pair of jeans every day, you should only wash them every three or four months as the washing and friction can make the jeans' colour fade. It is suggested that you should not wash jeans in washing machines or dry-clean them, as this destroys their original water-washed lines or creates some unexpected effects. After drying, jeans should not be exposed to the sun for too long, as the fabrics may oxidise, making the colours fade. Also, don't wash your jeans on a rainy day, or they may get mouldy.

Currently, jeans in the market are washed, polished and shaped by their designers. Though you may try to reshape them, their style remains mostly fixed. The only things you can do to modify them is to fade the colour in some parts of the jeans by using chemicals, make drawings on the jeans, use sandpaper to thin the fabric or simply cut holes in them with a pair scissors. It takes a long time for your own design to acquire a natural style that is shaped by wear and tear.

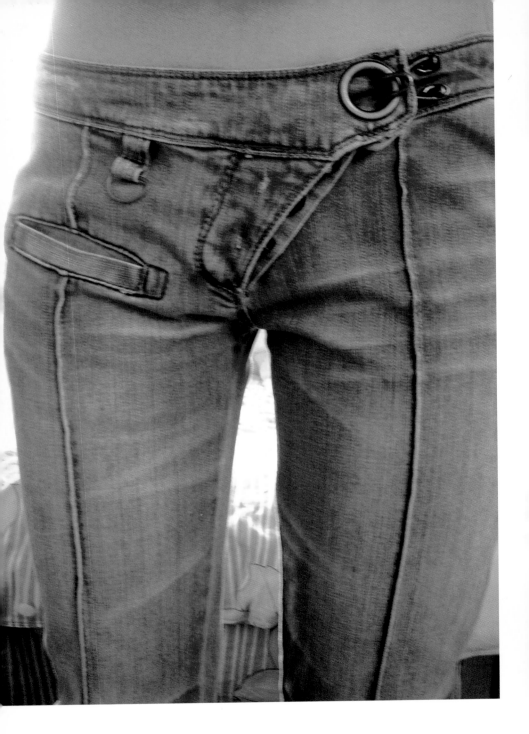

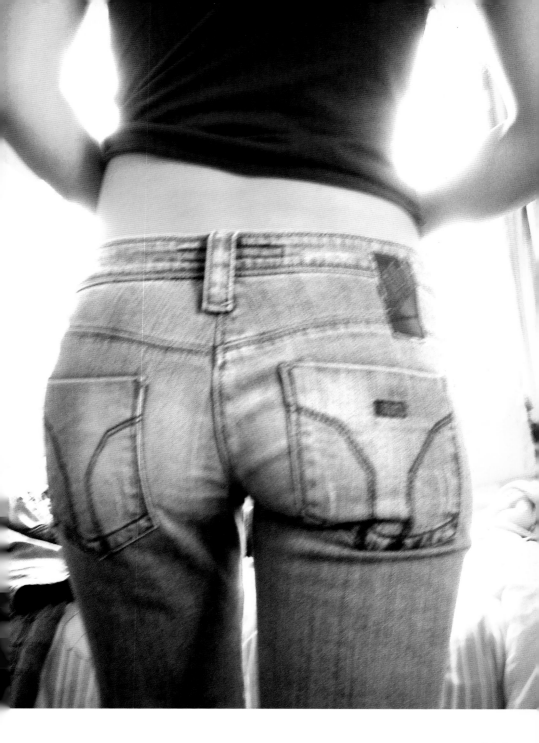

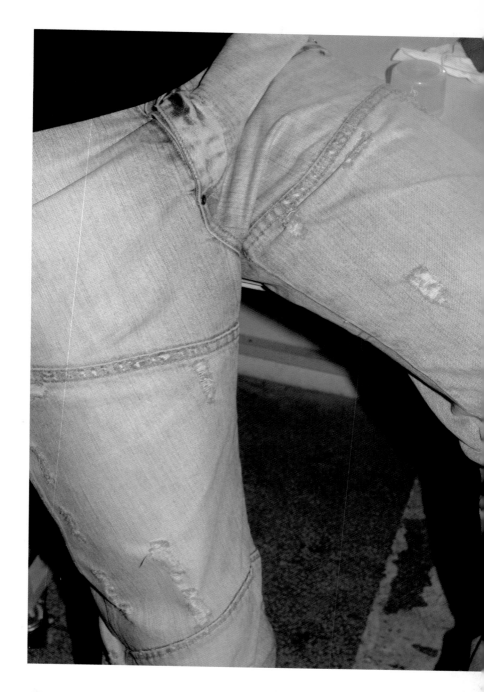